To my parents for letting us adopt a giant dog named Bandit

To my sister for not protesting

And to Bandit for teaching me the true magic of animals

STERLING CHILDREN'S BOOKS
New York

An Imprint of Sterling Publishing Co., Inc.
1166 Avenue of the Americas
New York, NY 10036

ISBN 978-1-4549-3089-1

Distributed in Canada by Sterling Publishing Co., Inc.
c/o Canadian Manda Group, 664 Annette Street
Toronto, Ontario M6S 2C8, Canada
Distributed in the United Kingdom by GMC Distribution Services
Castle Place, 166 High Street, Lewes, East Sussex BN7 1XU, England
Distributed in Australia by NewSouth Books
University of New South Wales, Sydney, NSW 2052, Australia

For information about custom editions, special sales, and premium and corporate purchases,
please contact Sterling Special Sales at 800-805-5489 or specialsales@sterlingpublishing.com.

Manufactured in China

Lot #:
2 4 6 8 10 9 7 5 3
11/18

sterlingpublishing.com

Cover and interior design by Heather Kelly

LIFE AT THE ZOO

THE SECRET WORLD OF YOUR FAVORITE ANIMALS

MICHAEL GEORGE

STERLING CHILDREN'S BOOKS

New York

king
penguin

INTRODUCTION

When you visit the animals at the zoo, you might see them eating, sleeping, or playing. But did you know these animals have a secret life that's not so different from yours? From babies to adults, zoo animals have a busy schedule! They go to school, the doctor, and even play games. Zookeepers, who are in charge of caring for the animals, get the animals where they need to go and keep them healthy and happy. These amazing humans learn everything they can to ensure animals live a long life!

Caring for zoo animals is not an easy task. All animals have different lifestyles and needs. Dolphins are highly intelligent and require a lot of attention. They want to play and **socialize**. Koalas, on the other hand, sleep for 18 hours a day. When they are awake, they don't mind being alone. Zookeepers usually specialize in a few types of animals, like birds, mammals, or amphibians. A single zookeeper may be in charge of one to three animal species' total care. While these animals have different needs, they all have to eat, and zookeepers are also in charge of mealtime. Large animals, like rhinoceroses, eat hundreds of pounds of food per day. Imagine trying to prepare that much food! Through teamwork, research, and a deep love for animals, zookeepers solve all kinds of problems.

Zookeepers work hard for their animals, but also because zoos are necessary to keep the planet's **wildlife** safe and protected. Many zoo animals are rescued and have nowhere else to go. Some scientists work with zoo animals to help understand and protect their animal relatives who live outside of captivity. Human activity is destroying the forests and oceans where many **species** live. By visiting zoos and all of your favorite animals, you support education and **conservation** programs that keep these beautiful creatures around for future generations.

ZOO BABIES

civets Kasih and Kamil ↗

So, where does life at the zoo begin? With the babies of course! Zoo babies may look small and cute, but they can be quite a handful! The little ones need to be taken care of 24 hours a day, with some being bottle-fed up to eight times! Sometimes, zookeepers develop a special bond with the newborns by taking them home when the zoo closes. That was the case for these two adorable civets named Kasih and Kamil. Though civets may look like cats, they are not felines. They are more closely related to weasels or mongooses. Civets are from Asia and Africa and live on a nocturnal schedule. That means they sleep all day, and are active at night. Imagine a baby civet running around your living room while you try to sleep! Kasih and Kamil are ten weeks old in this photo, and once full grown, they'll be close to three feet long. For now, they are so small you might find one napping in the hood of its keeper's jacket. As omnivores, civets like to eat both meat and plants. Because Kasih and Kamil are not very good at hunting (yet!), the keepers feed them small worms as a snack between bottle feedings.

Not all animals get to have sleepovers with their keepers. Aquatic animals cannot travel because they live in water that is set to the perfect temperature. These rescued baby manatees named José, Ursula, and Dex live in a **habitat** warmed to about 82 degrees Fahrenheit (28 degrees Celsius). In addition to their bottles, they love to munch on lettuce. These babies don't waste any food, and it takes up to seven days for a meal to travel through their digestive tract. These little guys look like they have a lot of baby fat, but they're *actually* just big-boned. Manatees only have 3 percent body fat! The rest of their curves are made up of bones and, as adults, they have up to one hundred and fifty feet of intestines. Once these babies are over six hundred pounds and close to seven feet long, they'll be ready to be released back into the wild.

manatees →
José, Ursula,
and Dex
↓

WHERE DO ZOO BABIES COME FROM?

People have the wrong idea about where animals in the zoo come from. They fear animals are stolen from the wild and that they are unhappy. But many animals, like Aku the walrus, were rescued from danger! Animals need help when they are separated from their families by storms, **natural disasters**, or when humans harm them or their homes. Without the zoo, these animals would likely not survive. Aku was found by gold miners in Alaska, separated from his mother and desperately in need of food and water. A rescue team brought him to Orlando and introduced Aku to another walrus calf named Ginger. Ginger was born in captivity to her parents Garfield and Kaboodle. The two walrus calves both love playing with fresh snow and their tiny red slide. They also love playing with the hose, which makes it a *little* hard for their keepers to clean up their habitat.

gentoo penguin

Other babies are born in the zoo as part of conservation breeding programs. When animals in the wild are **endangered**, they need help from humans. This penguin was hatched by an aviculturist as part of the Association of Zoos & Aquariums Species Survival Plan®. This program strives to save endangered animals. An aviculturist is what we call someone who raises and breeds birds. In the wild, animals choose their mates carefully, but animals don't have as many options in captivity.

Ginger the walrus

Aviculturists sometimes team up with scientists, working to move males and females between zoos. This way, animals do not accidentally mate with their relatives. This helps to keep the species healthy.

When babies are born at the zoo, the keepers do everything they can to ensure they grow up strong. For almost the entire first month of this gentoo penguin's life, he was hidden underneath his parents' tummies. Now, at six weeks old, he is being weighed to make sure he is healthy. In this photo, he weighs only three pounds, which is about as much as a toaster. That may not seem like much, but three pounds is a healthy weight for this little guy! He is on his way to growing into a big, strong fifteen-pound adult.

GOING TO SCHOOL!

lemur

T he zoo isn't just a walk in the park. As babies get older, they have to go to school. Rather than learning history or doing math homework, many animals learn to solve puzzles. This helps develop their brains. As the animals learn, zookeepers and scientists find out what drives their **behavior**. Have your parents ever convinced you to do something by using candy? Sugary foods get animals excited as well! Inside this plastic puzzle's drawers are delicious fruits. This lemur, named Bombo, can smell the fruit through the holes but he has to experiment to figure out how to get them. Over time, he learns to pull the drawers open instead of sticking his snout in the openings. You might be thinking: "That's so easy!" But if you had a lemur brain, you wouldn't see this as a simple task. From this puzzle, scientists can learn the age that lemurs start to problem solve.

Once we know how smart an animal is, we can create new research projects to learn more. These baby clouded leopards, Niran and Kuso, are full of **natural instincts** that they'll never lose. When given a dead mouse to eat, they will "stalk and kill it," even though it's already dead and ready to eat. Similar to housecats, these two are playful and spend their days wrestling around in the exhibit. They have a special joint in their ankle that allows them to rotate their paws and lock onto tree bark. With this ability, they can climb head first up or down a tree! As scientists observe zoo babies' behavior and **development**, they better understand what humans need to do to conserve and support the species in the wild. For example, if they discover Niran and Kuso need a certain tree species to make their home and survive, they can work to conserve that tree, which will in turn help to conserve the endangered clouded leopards.

clouded leopards
Niran and Kuso

Boone the panther

GROWING UP

When zoo babies are hand-raised, they're very comfortable around humans. Even so, they do not lose their natural instincts, which continue to develop as the animals mature. For carnivores, a safe distance must grow between the keeper and the animal. No matter how much the animal loves his keeper, he also loves meat, and those instincts cannot be controlled. Keepers begin to use whistles and other tools to continue training and strengthening their bond. This panther, named Boone, is being taught to stand up on his hind legs. This behavior allows the keeper to inspect his belly and assess his health. Boone was found and rescued as a cub from the Pacific Northwest, where he was being kept as an illegal pet. As a cougar kitten, Boone was just like your average housecat. He purred and meowed whenever he was hungry, and loved to playfully pounce. But, as he got older, those large teeth meant he could no longer "play bite." Boone and his keeper continue to grow their relationship, but they do it with a barrier to keep the keeper protected.

Separation is necessary for more than just humans' safety. Moving animals into a more natural habitat can help them learn to live on their own. Even animals have

eastern ↗ indigo snake

to grow up! This eastern indigo snake was recently moved from his indoor nursery to an outdoor enclosure. The outdoor enclosure is more like the wild, with local plants and a personal underground burrow. This snake is part of a conservation program, which means that in order to be released into the wild, it must first **adapt** to a natural setting that is controlled by the zoo. Over time, programs like this one can save endangered species. For animals that live in groups, like flamingoes and wolves, natural enclosures can help animals develop instincts before they join their larger zoo family. Otherwise, these animals risk being rejected by the herd.

TIME TO TRAIN

Zhu the red panda

As they grow, animals begin training to make a zookeeper's job easier. For example, how would you get a two-ton rhino to walk into the shower or inside its barn for the night? Most zoo animals are not like dogs. If you call their name or ask them to sit, they will ignore you. Instead, zookeepers use a tool called a **target** to show animals where they need them to go. Animals are taught to touch their nose, hand, trunk, or other body parts to the target. When they do this, the zookeeper presses a button that makes a clicking sound. Animals learn that the sight and sound of the target will get them a reward! This red panda named Zhu is being fed a raisin for successfully following the target. The keeper is moving Zhu out of his sleeping area and onto this branch in order to clean his bedding.

Target training is especially useful when working with larger animals, like these two alpacas. During their monthly health checkup, the alpacas need to be weighed. It's not easy getting a curious mammal to stand on a scale. Metal is not found in nature, so these two get spooked by it!

These young zookeepers, called Zooies, are enrolled in a boarding school that has its own zoo. Their assignment for the day was to weigh Birdie and Magnolia, and with a handful of food, they were successful! They had to be quick, because Magnolia doesn't like to stand still. Alpacas are adorable, but if they get angry or annoyed, they will spit in your face. How rude!

alpacas
Birdie and
Magnolia

Asian
elephants ↗

PLAYTIME

Zookeepers never want their animals to get bored, so they excite them by introducing new **stimulants** called "enrichment," which are meant to enhance an animal's life. Zookeepers bring out enrichment randomly to encourage natural behavior. For a rhino, enrichment can be a big yellow barrel it can balance on its horn. For a tiger, enrichment is a new smell or spice sprayed around the **exhibit**. For these elephants, enrichment is a surprise visit from their keeper to be fed a new fruit. Items such as piñatas, toys, scratching posts, and puzzles give animals the excitement of exploration while living in captivity. When you live at the zoo, you never know when a present might appear!

Social animals, like this giraffe named Jyoti, enjoy meeting new human visitors. Getting fed and introduced to people provides enrichment every day. You might be wondering, doesn't a long neck like that get in the way? Actually, no! Their long necks give giraffes access to the juiciest leaves on the trees, about 16 to 20 feet above the ground. Giraffes love leaves and lettuce, and their long purple tongues can wrap around almost anything. Thanks to their necks, giraffes hold the record as the world's tallest land mammals.

Jyoti the giraffe →

This photo showcases a special program where visitors get to take over snack time. In order to feed these giraffes, humans need a little help, so this zoo built a platform to bring visitors to the height of a tree. Remember, you should never feed animals at the zoo unless a staff member is with you and has given permission!

ZOO GROWN-UPS

← PJ the rhinoceros

When animals reach adulthood, their brains are fully developed and their instincts have kicked in. It's their time to thrive! Living in the zoo has many benefits, including a longer lifespan. In the wild, animals face food shortages, **predators**, harsh **climates**, and competition. At the zoo, life is much less stressful! Animals are fed healthy, whole-food diets that do not include any processed ingredients. They are constantly pampered, like this rhino named PJ. Twice a week he receives a horn and toenail rubdown with a mineral oil that prevents the hard outer layers from cracking. His horn is made from keratin, the same material as your hair! Rhinos have a bad reputation of being aggressive, but the truth is, they have poor eyesight and are easily scared. They end up charging at anything they hear, but can't see. Despite looking sluggish, PJ can run up to 30–35 miles per hour.

As animals grow up, zookeepers learn their unique personalities. Although zoo animals interact with humans their entire lives, many species hold onto their wild side. You don't want to get close to an animal with an unreliable temper.

This muntjac deer named Xiao is known for being super friendly. When animals are naturally kind, they will be chosen for special roles at the zoo (like this photo shoot!). Xiao has a baby face, a gentle presence, and loves eating apples. Despite his youthful features and small size, you can tell he is a full-grown adult by his horns. The tallest a muntjac can grow is only 1.7 feet! Muntjac are the oldest species of deer, and have existed on Earth for at least twenty million years. They bark like dogs when disturbed, and have long tongues they use to strip leaves off branches.

Xiao the deer

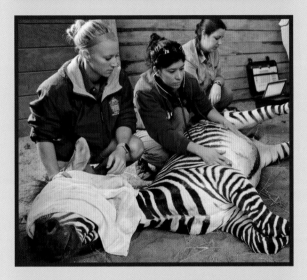

Ruuxa
the zebra

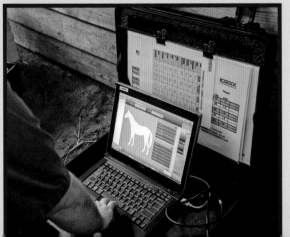

MEDICAL CARE

Every zoo has a **veterinarian** on staff to help the animals when they get sick. These animal doctors are specially trained to deal with a wide range of species. If you think a human doctor's job is hard, imagine having a patient that cannot tell you what's wrong or where it hurts! Zookeepers are very observant and always report unusual changes in animal behavior to the vet. This zebra named Ruuxa was walking funny, and his keepers discovered he had a fractured leg. Don't worry! After a successful surgery, our striped friend was given an X-ray to check on the healing process, and now he's back in tip-top shape! During this appointment, veterinarians tested his heart rate and trimmed his hooves so they did not overgrow or split. Ruuxa was lying down because many animals are frightened by doctors and needles (just like humans!). He must be perfectly still during complicated appointments. If there is a danger to the zookeeper, or if the animal must be still for longer than a few minutes, they will be given medicine that puts them to sleep for a little while.

It doesn't matter how small you are, every animal in the zoo goes to the doctor. Even the amphibians and reptiles! Zoo vets have tools in many different sizes, like this extra, extra small heart monitor. This bullfrog,

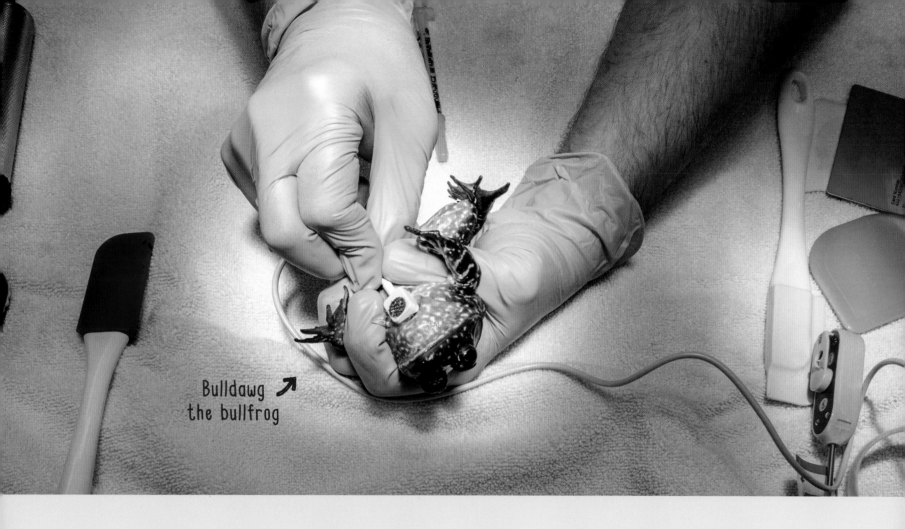

Bulldawg → the bullfrog

named Bulldawg, was brought in when the **ultraviolet light** in his cage burned out. The UV light mimics the sun. The light provides Bulldawg with important nutrients, like Vitamin D, which helps him absorb **calcium**. After being weighed, examined, and having his blood drawn, he was back to hopping around! When injuries happen in nature, animals have a hard time recovering. Easy access to the doctor is another reason animals live longer in zoos than in the wild!

harbor
seals

ANIMAL AMBASSADORS

Zoo animals that are kind and intelligent get the chance to interact directly with visitors! Animal shows provide entertainment for guests and allow the animals to exercise their bodies and brains. Animal ambassadors are naturally social and are trained using only **positive reinforcement**. All of their performance behaviors are **voluntary** and may take many forms: Dolphins jump and flip through the air, owls soar above your head without making a sound, and seals can give you a high five! Seals are super smart and have the ability to learn dozens of tricks. Unlike humans, they save oxygen in their muscles instead of their lungs. This allows them to stay underwater for up to half an hour! Although they are graceful in the water, on land they move like blubbery caterpillars. Their zookeeper trains them using a high-pitched whistle. This unique sound stands out from all the other noises at the zoo and tells the seals when they have done a good job. As you can see here, seals also like to give wet kisses.

In addition to shows, other animals become ambassadors and go on field trips outside the zoo. They travel to schools, parks, and community centers to help teach people about wildlife and conservation. Animal ambassadors have to be thoroughly trained, and their daily classes strengthen their relationship with their keeper. Positive reinforcement means they are only rewarded for doing something good, and never punished for doing something bad. This type of training helps the animals view humans as friends! Even though animals are sometimes on a leash, they are never pulled along. These animals want to perform, because they know they'll get food—and showcasing their natural talents is much easier and less stressful than hunting in the wild. This Harris's Hawk, named Onyx, can join you on a walk in the woods to showcase how he flies in a natural environment. Onyx only weighs 1.5 pounds and flies fast and low. Even though Onyx is free to fly away, he always returns to his falconer because of their close relationship.

Onyx
the hawk

CONCLUSION

bearcats Wilbur
and Willow

Zookeepers and animals often work together for decades, from when the animals are born to when they grow old. Alison has worked with these bearcats, Wilbur and Willow, for a few years now. They love walking on her shoulders, and treat her like a tree! Bearcats have a surprising and special secret: They smell like popcorn. Sadly, this magically scented animal is slowly disappearing from the world. Because of **climate change** and human activity, the bearcat's wild habitat in southern Asia is shrinking. The population is declining at a rate of 30 percent over the last 18 years. We need zoos to connect people with endangered animals, to help them understand these problems and to inspire the need for protection.

The Galápagos tortoise is a rare success story. Through education and conservation efforts, this once endangered population is on the rise! Abrazo is over 115 years old and came to the United States in 1928. He has lived long enough to see his species saved! But you better not try and pick him up to congratulate him, because he weighs as much as a grand piano. He does enjoy a good scratch though, and as a natural response will stop moving completely, as if he's playing freeze tag.

Life at the zoo for Abrazo and other animals is rich with activity. Behind the scenes, zookeepers are always working to provide enrichment, education, medical treatment, training, and more. Next time you visit the zoo, be sure to thank the staff for everything they do to provide the animals with a wonderful life. Now that you have discovered the secret world of your favorite animals, be sure to tell your friends that life at the zoo is much more than it appears for these amazing animals!

Abrazo the
Galápagos tortoise

ABOUT THE AUTHOR

MICHAEL GEORGE is a photographer, writer, and animal lover based out of Brooklyn, New York. In his work he strives to tell meaningful stories about travel, nature, and underrepresented communities. His work has been published in *National Geographic*, *The New York Times*, *Teen Vogue*, and dozens of other international publications. *Life at the Zoo* is his first book. His favorite part of working on this project was when he played with two baby walruses and discovered they act like puppies.

This book would not be possible without all of the incredible zookeepers, veterinarians, and staff that graciously volunteered their time and energy. A heartfelt thank you to the following zoos:

- Riverbanks Zoo & Garden in Columbia, South Carolina (pages 2-3, 27, back cover)
- Tierpark Berlin & Zoo Berlin in Berlin, Germany (pages 18, 24-25, back cover)
- Nashville Zoo at Grassmere in Nashville, Tennessee (pages 8, 13, 26, back cover)
- The Trevor Zoo at the Millbrook School in Millbrook, New York (pages 12, 16-17, 21, back cover)
- Central Florida Zoo and Botanical Gardens in Sanford, Florida (pages 14, 20, 23)
- Orianne Center for Indigo Conservation in Eustis, Florida (page 15)
- SeaWorld and their Animal Rescue Team in Orlando, Florida (cover, pages 5-6, 8-11, 30-31)
- ZooTampa at Lowry Park in Tampa, Florida (pages 7, 19, 22, back cover)

GLOSSARY

Adapt—to change because of a different environment or situation.

Behavior—the specific way an animal acts.

Calcium—a chemical that is important for healthy teeth and bones.

Climate—the weather of a place over a long period of time.

Climate change—changes to weather, including global warming, caused by human activity.

Conservation—the act of protecting wildlife, natural resources, or environments.

Development—natural growth to a more mature state.

Endangered species—a plant or animal in danger of no longer existing, usually because of human activity.

Exhibit—a public display showcasing animals or an environment.

Habitat—where animals or plants are usually found.

Natural disasters—an event in nature, such as an earthquake, tornado, or flood, that causes damage.

Natural instincts—the pattern of behavior or actions shared by a specific animal species.

Positive reinforcement—rewards given out to encourage animals to repeat a desired behavior.

Predators—animals that hunt other animals for food.

Socialize—to be friendly and enjoy the company of others.

Species—one of the groups used to divide animals (or plants).

Stimulants—a substance, object, or situation that encourages growth, development, or activity.

Target—a tool used by zookeepers to show animals where they need to go.

Veterinarian—a doctor who is trained to treat animals.

Voluntary—an action that is done willingly or without force.

Ultraviolet light—a type of light, given off by the sun, that causes tans and cannot be seen by the human eye.

Wildlife—animals living in a natural environment.